The Conference Companion
Sketchnotes, Doodles, and Creative Play
for Teaching and Learning

©2017 Illustrated and written by Becky Green

All rights reserved. No part of this publication may be reproduced in any form or by any electronic or mechanical means, including information storage and retrieval systems, without permission in writing by the publisher, except by a reviewer who may quote brief passages in a review. For information regarding permission, contact the publisher at press@raisingamaker.com.

These books are available at special discounts when purchased in quantity for use as premiums, promotions, fundraising, and educational use. For inquiries and details, contact the publisher: press@raisingamaker.com.

Published by Raising A Maker
Editing and Interior Design by My Writers' Connection
Cover Design by Becky Green

Library of Congress Control Number: 2019916404
Paperback ISBN: 978-1-7341444-2-0

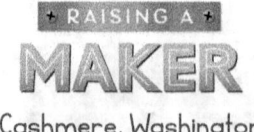

Cashmere, Washington

The Conference Companion

Sketchnotes, Doodles, and Creative Play for Teaching and Learning

Becky Green

Table of Contents

What's This Book All About? vii
I Solemnly Swear: Commitments for Creatives ix

Sketchnote Basics 1
Speech Bubbles
Lightbulbs
Arrows
Fonts and Lettering
People

At the Conference 13
Dig Into Your Toolbox
The Tools in Action
Try It Out
Session Notes

While You're Sitting There 34
Places
Food
People Take Two
Observations
Fonts Take Two
Bingo
Connections
Doodle a Day
Quotes
Contacts
Notes

Back to the Classroom 62

More from Raising A Maker 66
About the Author 69

What's This Book All About?

This notebook offers lessons and practice on how to take what you hear and turn it into something you'll remember and--gasp--maybe even use. These pages share the basics of creating and using shapes, doodles, and letters to form helpful sketchnotes that record and organize ideas. This is a space for wobbly lines. And trying new things. And making mistakes. And learning playfully.

Practically speaking, this notebook will show you options for taking notes, capturing learning, and enjoying your time. If you're sitting at a conference, seminar, or meeting--you will put these activities into practice.

Hopefully speaking, this book will help you think more deeply, playfully, and creatively. If you're sitting at home, you'll find activities that get your pen moving.

Educator-ly speaking, this book will give you light-hearted fodder for your classrooms and the listeners and thinkers who fill those good learning spaces. If you're sitting at school, you'll find an activity or twenty to try with your kiddos.

I Solemnly Swear

(and not just under my breath)

Commitments for Creatives:

- There is no "bad drawing." There is drawing in my inspired style and my inspired way.

- There is no singular "right way" to do activities in this book.

- Anything is inspiration: my neighbor's tattoo, the design of the bathroom tiles, the swirl on the dry faculty lounge cookie. They are my fodder for greatness. Or at least amusement.

- I try. I make messes. I applaud mistakes.

- I channel my six-year-old self who hung art on the refrigerator without fear. I roll my eyes only once a page and do not self-deprecate my doodles.

- I have permission to steal doodle ideas. To copy. To replicate what I see. To look over my neighbor's shoulder (until they tell me I'm being creepy).

- I let myself play. Adults get to be creative. Grown-ups get to have fun. Teachers can draw too.

The Basics

Let's start filling your sketchnote toolbox. These tools are simply the basics. Whether this is your first time doodling since your age was in the single digits, or you are a master artist, there is benefit from practicing, learning, and personalizing the basics of sketchnoting. The shapes on the next pages can turn what you hear into insights you'll remember, use, and share. Ready to play?

Speech Bubbles

Rectangles, triangles, ovals, and any other shape can become a speech bubble.

See what happened there? Just put two shapes together!

Shapes convey a tone. Use a shape that matches the message.

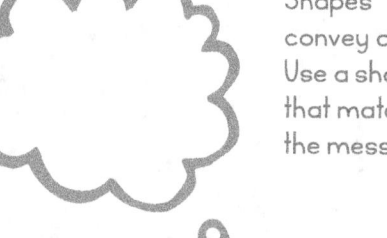

Why do speech bubbles matter? They help you find quotes on a page, capture thoughts you want to consider, and draw attention to the most important messages. What did the speaker say that made your jaw drop? Put it in a bubble!

How can a bold bubble line match a bold statement?

Doodle your own features and thought bubble. What are you wondering right now?

Lightbulbs

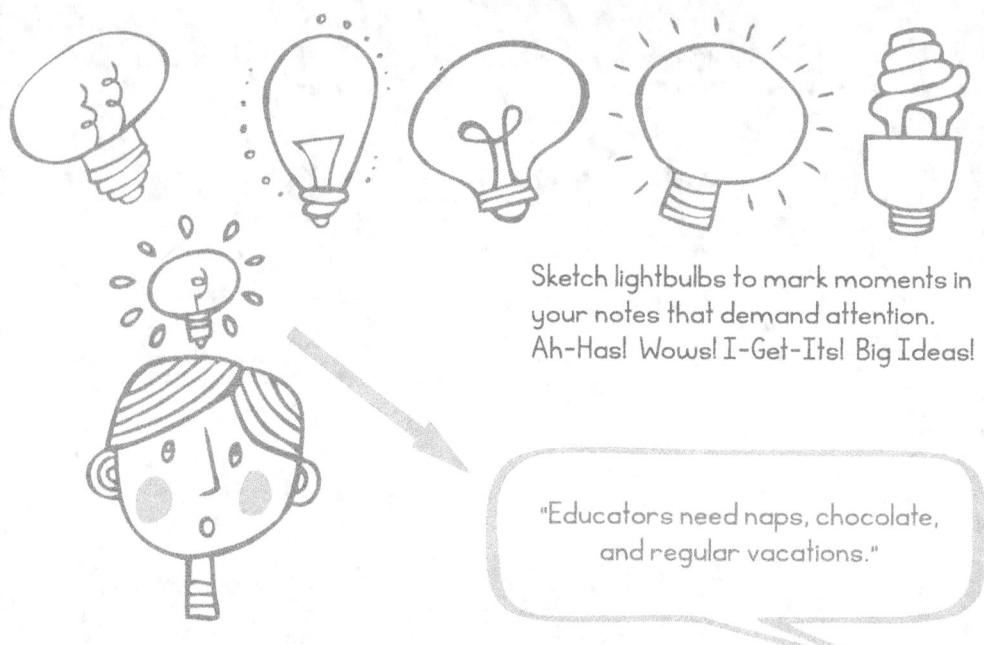

Sketch lightbulbs to mark moments in your notes that demand attention. Ah-Has! Wows! I-Get-Its! Big Ideas!

"Educators need naps, chocolate, and regular vacations."

Lightbulbs (like everything) are just shapes and squiggles.

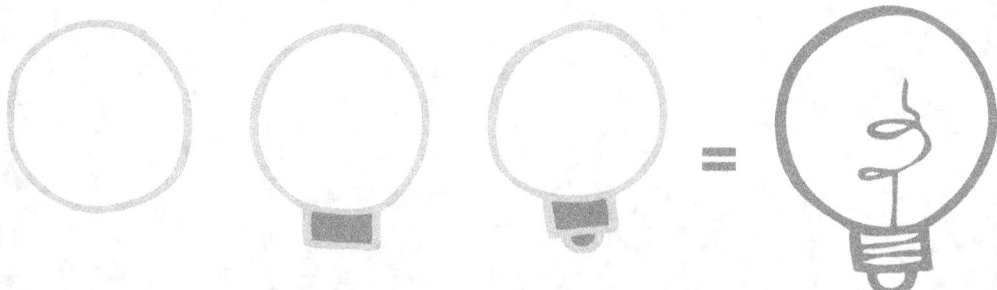

Add dots, lightning bolts, triangles, and lines for emphasis. Draw shapes to draw attention.

Practice your own lightbulbs to mark great ideas.

Doodle Boo's big brainstorm.

Arrows

Arrows help you connect ideas, direct the flow of a speaker's points, and clarify jumbled ideas.

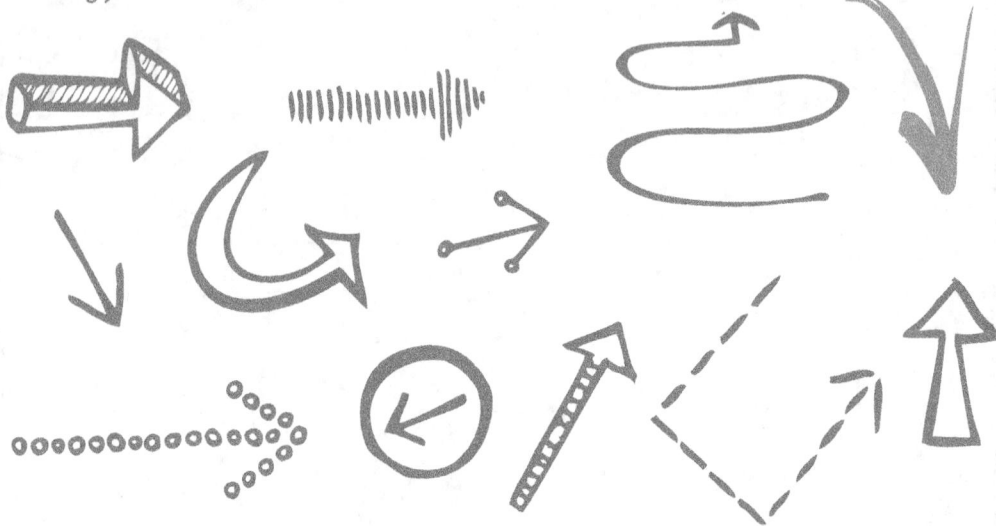

There is no wrong way to draw an arrow. Lines, dots, squiggles, and dashes can all help clear up confusion or point to important ideas on a page.

When you read back through your notes, arrows should help you know what matters.

Arrows help us notice and navigate. Label each rectangle with the events of your ideal day—out of order. Then practice doodling a variety of arrow styles to connect the moments chronologically.

Fonts and Lettering

How you choose to write words can create as much meaning as the words themselves. The tools you choose will impact the tone and design of the notes you take. Select a favorite pen or pencil, and play with letters.

Making simple font styles is as easy as drawing lines.

Add an extra line to turn plain letters into a style. Thicken one line for a new look. Get crazy and add more lines or random dots. Now you're a typographer!

You can also make letters from simple shapes.

    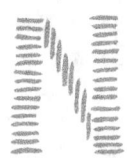

(Maybe not mix TOO many ideas)

And then mix shapes and lines to create more fonts.

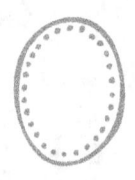    

 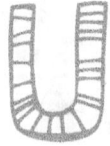     

Try out your own fonts.
Need word ideas?

Your name
Your gradeschool nickname
First pet
The country you're in
Last book title you read
Your first phone number
Your sixth-grade math teacher

People

People are just shapes with a few defining features.
Start with a shape and then add a few more (wobbly lines encouraged).

Think about features you can exaggerate and turn into a shape.

Look around the room and add details to blank faces. What shape is your neighbor's head?

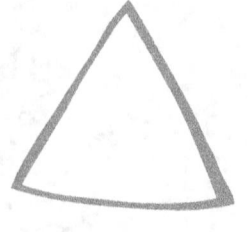 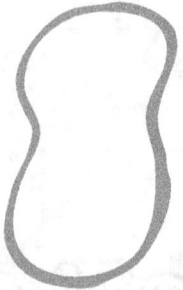  

Try out your own faces. Look for different shapes in the crowd.

Add features to these folks.

At the Conference

(or faculty meeting or seminar or while people-watching at the coffee shop. Use the pages to capture new learnings, pass the time, and play.)

> Repetitive doodles help you think. Fill the margins. Use blank space to draw.

Build Your Toolbox

Whether you're at the morning keynote of a multi-day conference, sitting in a workshop session, or watching a video in a faculty meeting, there are ideas to capture, use, and consider. It's time to use the doodle tools you've already learned and add to your collection.

Images can point to tweets, websites, movies, people, book titles, articles, thoughts, questions, and more. What doodles will direct your thinking? What symbols will you use?

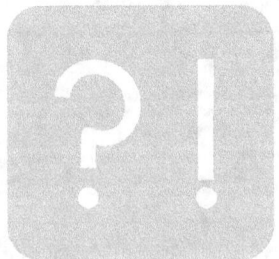

The Tools in Action

While listening to a speaker (Dr. Doodleguru), sketchnotes create a visual that helps you record and synthesize.

What could notes look like?

LUNCH at 11:30 IN THE ATRIUM

@dgguru

Dr. Doodleguru

DEVOTING 10 MIN TO doodling = MORE learning all day long.

REPETITIVE doodles can unlock NEW, INNOVATIVE THOUGHTS!

IT'S NOT about aesthetics. IT'S about the attention to an idea.

DRAWING IS THINKING. IT slows us down. Before difficult tasks— DRAW.

SCRATCH PAPER ON EVERY desk

Remember: there is no right way. There is only your way.

The Daily Create
Sharpie Gallery
Atlantic Article: "Cognitive Benefits of Doodling"

- Skill has no effect on power of doodling
- Small areas to draw on feel safer (cut squares of paper)
- Graphics are hardwired in humans. Before writing— visual literacy
- Doodling boosts executive functions. Doodling = INTERVENTION?

PICTURE THIS by Lynda Barry

+ZENTANGLE
+Doodle REVOLUTION

Watch Helvetica

Doodlers find it 29% easier to recall info!

ASK PEOPLE, "WHEN DID YOU STOP DRAWING? WHY?"

TRY white gel pen on black ink. How does working with negative space = BIG ideas?

Try It Out

While listening to a speaker (or podcast, online tutorial, or boring phone call), consider if a page with more structure helps you collect ideas or if you thrive on a blank slate. Try both out on these two pages.

Don't forget our creative commitments. Yes, you CAN draw!

Must-watch

Who is the speaker?

Big ideas to remember

Tweets

Must-reads

Websites

Did you use fonts for tone? Thought bubbles? Speech bubbles?

Session Notes

Whether you're in a keynote, a classroom, or a quick meeting—the tools you've just practiced can be put together in creative ways. Use the following pages to try them out.

> Create a symbol for contact info. What's the speaker's email?

Session Notes

Research? Key ideas? Questions? Topics to investigate?
Let symbols direct your next steps.

Session Notes

How will you mark something worth celebrating? What symbol resonates?

Session Notes

What other symbols do you need to create? Make your own!

Don't forget!

Ooh! Great tool for the classroom!

Others need to hear this!

Session Notes

Meeting people? Choose a
communication symbol to mark
contact info you collect today.

Session Notes

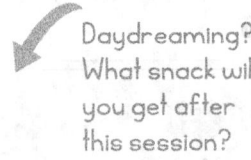

Daydreaming? What snack will you get after this session?

Session Notes

Attention waning? Repetitive doodles help us refocus and listen. Look around the room. Do you see a pattern on someone's shirt you can replicate in this box?

Session Notes

Do boxes help you order your thoughts? There's a reason outlines help writers draft. See what happens when you add boxes to a page.

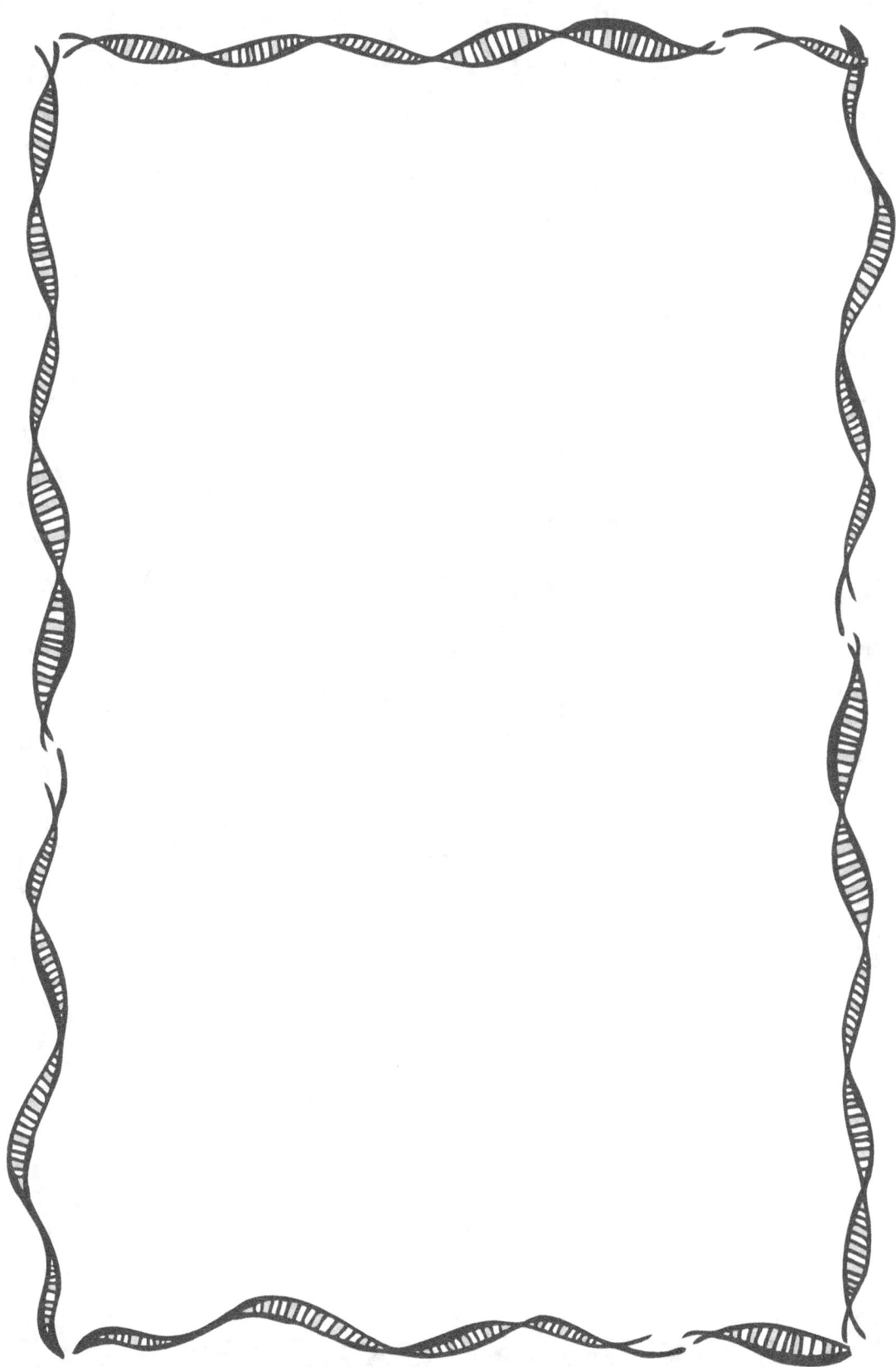

While You're Sitting There...

Taking notes to capture learning matters. So does creativity and an inspired mind. During breaks, lunch, and after listening, consider the creative prompts that follow to enhance your experience, build community, grow your doodle skills, and have some creative fun.

It's Possible That...

Doodle a border for this page.

> Doodling helps you pay attention and synthesize new concepts.

> Exercises in creativity open your mind to new ideas and unlock the potential for greater learning.

> Play is an essential component of the learning process (learners laugh too).

> Doodling is an enjoyable way to spend some time, to capture experiences, and to celebrate experiences.

> Apply our creative commitments and try out the following pages of exercises. Take some back to the classroom!

Images of Place

can make fantastic doodles.

Patterns

Fauna

Symbols

Buildings

Flora

Look around. What textiles, patterns, and shapes do you see? What trees did you pass this morning? What design is on your coffee mug?

Things

Vehicles

Landmarks
make great doodles too!

What landmarks, sculptures, or buildings are special to the place you are in now?

Just like faces, buildings are only shapes put together. Try out your own images of places.

Play with Your Food

Food sometimes makes the best doodles and the best creative fuel. What we eat and drink holds memories and generates stories.

Serve yourself some ice cream.

Just like faces, food starts as shapes.

Food has patterns we can steal and repeat.

    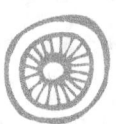 

What's in these cups?

What's between these buns?

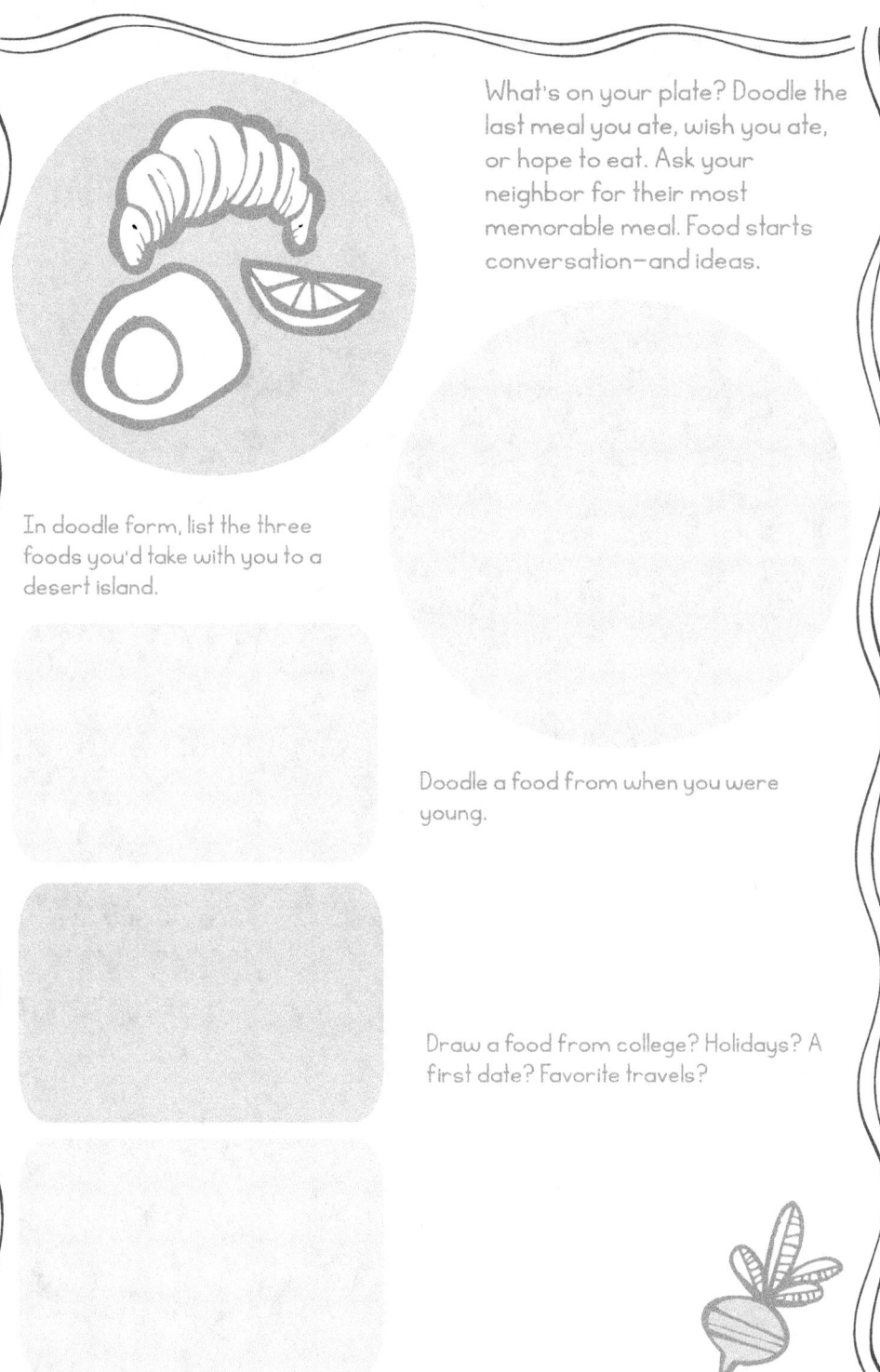

What's on your plate? Doodle the last meal you ate, wish you ate, or hope to eat. Ask your neighbor for their most memorable meal. Food starts conversation—and ideas.

In doodle form, list the three foods you'd take with you to a desert island.

Doodle a food from when you were young.

Draw a food from college? Holidays? A first date? Favorite travels?

Observations = Art

Art is all around you. What do you see that is ordinary? Boring? Surprising? Kooky? Familiar? Everything is fodder for a doodle that could hold your attention and/or lead to other ideas.

Do you see a carpet, scarf, or other fabric pattern? Turn it into simple shapes and doodle it. Can you make a repeating design?

Scan the room. What features do you see that you can mix and match into a unique face?

Observe and draw objects. Coffee mugs, shoes, eyeglasses, pencils, and key chains make good art. Embellish on the ordinary.

Design a postage stamp for the city you're in.

Turn an ordinary boot into a wild one.

Coffee? Tea? Or cocoa?

People Take Two

Let's draw some more faces.

Invent hats and hairstyles.

Add faces.

Extend your skills to robot faces.

And monsters.

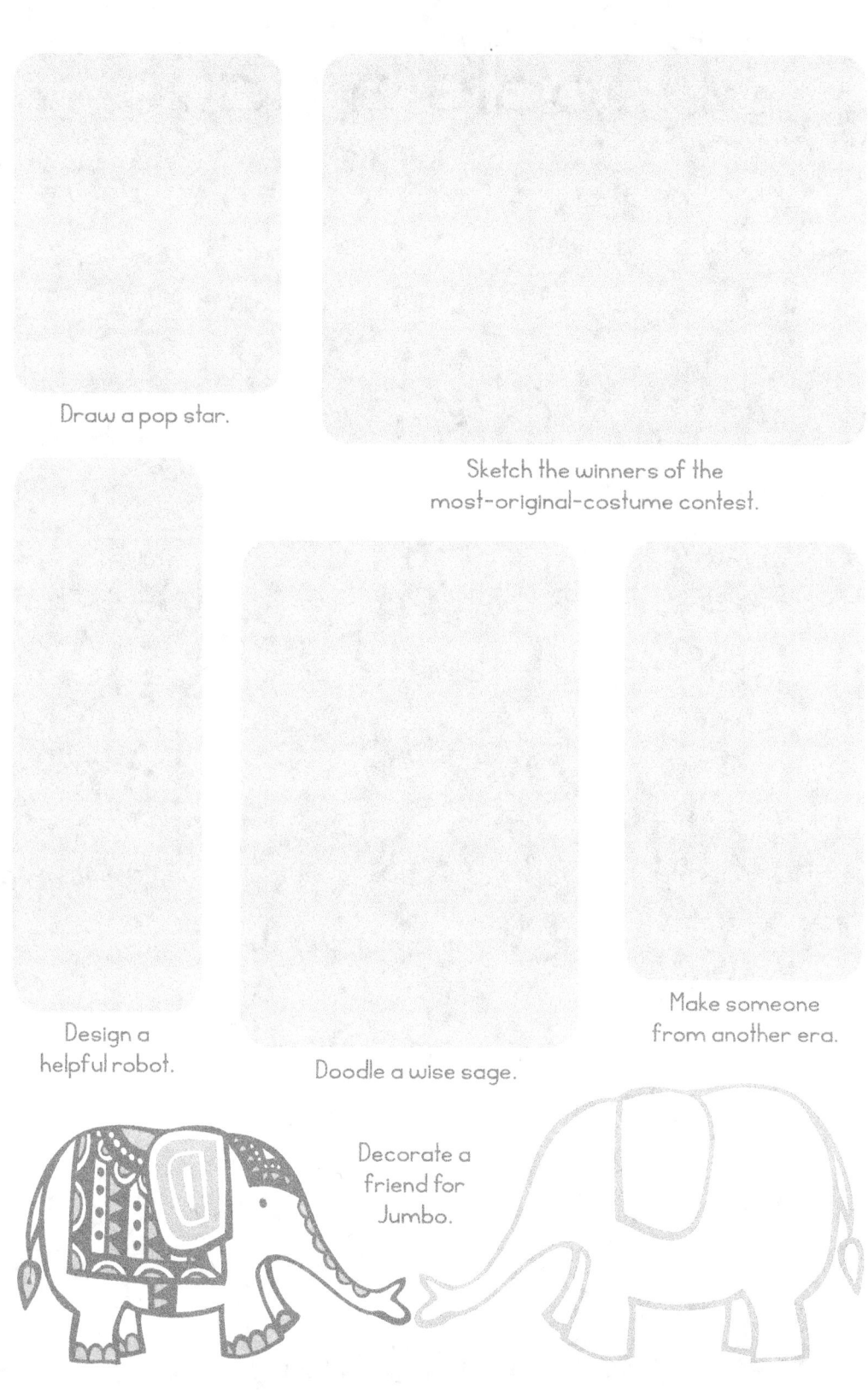

Draw a pop star.

Sketch the winners of the most-original-costume contest.

Design a helpful robot.

Doodle a wise sage.

Make someone from another era.

Decorate a friend for Jumbo.

Doodle a Day

by ZYV8ORb

TRAFFIC jam on the STAR way

DINNER. MMMM...

WeATHER

♪ ...FOR here AM I SITTING IN a TIN CAN FAR above THE WORLD ♪

WHERE ARE MY SAUCER KEYS???

⭐︎🔫 = ?

ZRb Ball with GG1X!

GREAT book!

STARbeaker JUICE

WALKED PAST THE XQ8*X TOWERS

How can drawing our days build community in a classroom?

44

Now, Your Day

Today's Weather

You

What did you see, smell, taste, touch, hear?

Whom did you talk to?

What did you learn?

What did you worry about? Laugh over?

Landmarks and Buildings

Food

Fonts Take Two

Let's play with letters some more! Handwriting helps us remember what we write and helps us capture phrases with tone. It can be as simple as starting with plain letters.

letters

Take a word and just add an extra outline. Now you have a funky font. There's no wrong way to do this.

letters

WORDS

Start from plain letters again. Add a few leaves here and there and some triangles at the bases of straight lines. Words turn into art.

WORDS

script

Script

What if you just thicken lines and add a few crumbs?

Script

Outline

Color in backgrounds.
Explore negative space.
Fill the page with fonts!

Embellish your letters. Use pens of different thicknesses. Experiment.

Conference Alphabet

Now put your creative lettering skills to work. From A to Z, list a word related to your conference learning, experience, and observations. Capture your highlights in alphabet form while trying out new doodle styles.

A

H

N

Q

T

X

How might your students use alphabets to recall learnings?

Z

How might you celebrate or roast a friend with an alphabet? Record a memory?

Conference Numbers

Decorate the numbers and doodle the ones that are missing. What have you experienced or seen today that these numbers match?

1 2 3
4 5
7 9

Record the numbers! How many new people did you meet today? How many tote bags with apples on them did you spy? How many countries are attendees from? How many slides in the keynote? Count something around you.

Let's Play Conference Bingo!

Mark off what you observe and experience. How fast can you get four in a row? A blackout?

conference freebies	line to use the bathroom	typo	the word "meta"
reluctant filling of first row	groovy tattoo	obnoxious verbal filler	elevator music
pop culture reference	person that looks 80% like a celebrity	squeaky chair	twitter/hashtag mention
tote bag	a phone not on silent	somebody doodling	book you want to read

Now, using your amazing doodling skills, pick one of those to draw.

Make Your Own Bingo

The possibilities are endless. Faculty meeting Bingo? Coffee shop Bingo? Long phone call with your in-laws Bingo? Parent conference Bingo? Doodle-your-day Bingo? Use images and words to personalize your own Bingo card.

Conference Connections

Draw your neighbor's sock/shirt/tie/jewelry pattern.

Offer your neighbor a mint. Draw the mint. Or a cupcake.

Draw a landmark from your hometown. What landmark would your neighbor draw?

Feeling Gregarious?

Find someone who has been to your college town.

Figure out two things the people on both sides of you have in common.

Draw your neighbors' names with your non-dominant hand.

Ask someone what song they listened to on repeat in the seventh grade.

Put your new acquaintances on the map.

Conversation

Introvert? Extrovert? Whether you're someone who needs talking points or has words to share, conversation starters are creative fodder. Use these starters, make some doodle starters, and avoid (or draw through) the awkward silence that comes from sitting at tables with strangers.

- What did you used to draw on your binder as a kid?
- Last book/movie/meme/song that you couldn't stop talking about?
- Best city you ever lived in?
- What is something you do badly?
- Favorite teacher?
- Story of the first car/bike/roller skates/Segway you ever owned?
- What's your secret agent name? (It's your middle name + the last food you ate.)
- If you had your choice of any beverage at this exact moment—what would you choose and why?
- Memorable piece of advice you've received?
- What's something new you want to learn to do?

Fill the Page

Take what you know and fill a page with doodles, designs, and patterns. Try it out.

Quotes

Doodling the most important messages of your day (or life) helps you think about them, apply them, and remember them. Fill these pages with memorable messages.

"We are visual creatures. When you doodle an image that captures the essence of an idea, you not only remember it, but you also help other people understand and act on it." —Tom Wujec

"Wisdom begins in wonder."
—Socrates

Contacts

Conferences are about connecting. Use these pages to record contacts, tape in business cards, and save your next Twitter contact.

Any faces from today you don't want to forget?

Notes

Notes

Back to the Classroom

You've doodled. You've taken notes. You've put symbols and fonts and drawings together to capture new ideas. What now?

This book is a reference for your learnings and your future sketchnoting adventures, but it should also inspire classrooms. Here are some ideas for you and your students:

Turn Bingo into a study tool. Have students fill squares with essential concepts and collaborate throughout the room, looking for classmates who can explain concepts to give them four in a row.

Turn Bingo into a get-to-know-you mixer. Fill each square with an experience or quality (pet owner, gum-chewer, bubble tea fanatic) and let students mingle, crossing off squares that apply to them.

Ask writing students to draw their characters' days for more insights on how to develop characters.

Start class by drawing your days and look for commonalities, talking points, and connections that build community.

Teach students repetitive doodles or symbols to draw when they feel stuck, are pondering, or need to step away from a challenging task. Doodles revive thinking.

Create a jar of class "conversation starters." Start each day by drawing from the jar and encouraging partner talk on unique topics.

Build vocabulary power through images. Draw symbols and pictures on cards rather than words to create memory triggers for tough concepts.

Teach students the basics: speech bubbles, arrows, lightbulbs, etc. Have them try out new note-taking methods to find the system that fits their learning styles best.

Ask students to sketchnote a partner's recorded practice presentation. Reviewing each other's doodles may help them see concepts that are clear and areas for revision.

Keep squares of scratch paper on desks for quick doodles when student attention is waning.

Have students storyboard ideas in symbols and images as they plan drafts, presentations, and projects.

Celebrate learning and student insights by keeping a "doodle wall" where students post inspiring and humorous quotes from one another and their studies. Teach fonts to give the wall tone.

Keep a map of the world on the wall where students doodle their travels, dream-travels, memorable meals, past and future homes, and other global connections.

Keep new vocabulary words in a jar. Draw them out randomly and ask students to speed doodle definitions in images only. Use these doodles as visual flashcards for further study.

Model the basics of drawing faces. Have students sketch quick self-portraits that reflect their moods and wonderings. Pass out blank outlines of faces and create student-drawn emoticons to support, encourage, and share the affective pulse of your group.

Create a class alphabet as a community builder. How can each letter reflect something special about every student?

Start a weekly "class by the numbers." Celebrate student growth by sharing out stats about student kindnesses, extra-curricular victories, and interests.

Doodle. Just doodle. And see where those drawings take you.

More Books From Raising A Maker
raisingamaker.com

50 Ways to Use YouTube in the Classroom
By Patrick Green
YouTubeClassroom.com

Your students are already accessing YouTube, so why not meet them where they are as consumers of information? By using the tools they choose, you can maximize their understanding in ways that matter. *50 Ways to Use YouTube in the Classroom* is an accessible guide that will improve your teaching, your students' learning, and your classroom culture.

Classroom Management in the Digital Age
Effective Practices for Technology-Rich Learning Spaces
By Patrick Green and Heather Dowd
CMDigitalAge.com

Classroom Management in the Digital Age helps guide and support teachers through the new landscape of device-rich classrooms. It provides practical strategies to novice and expert educators alike who want to maximize learning and minimize distraction. Learn how to keep up with the times while limiting time wasters and senseless screen-staring time.

More Books From Grafo House
grafohousepublishing.com

Manejo del Salón de Clase en la Era Digital
Prácticas Efectivas para Espacios de Aprendizaje Ricos en Tecnología
Por Patrick Green y Heather Dowd
CMDigitalAge.com

Manejo del Salón de Clase en la Era Digital ayuda a guiar y apoyar a los docentes a través del nuevo panorama de aulas con dispositivos. Proporciona estrategias prácticas para educadores novatos y expertos que desean maximizar el aprendizaje y minimizar la distracción. Aprenda cómo mantenerse actualizado, limitando el tiempo desperdiciado en las lecciones y el tiempo en la pantallas sin sentido.

Transforming Libraries
A Toolkit for Innovators, Makers, and Seekers
By Ron Starker

In the Digital Age, it's more important than ever for libraries to evolve into gathering points for collaboration, spaces for innovation, and places where authentic learning occurs. In *Transforming Libraries*, Ron Starker reveals ways to make libraries makerspaces, innovation centers, community commons, and learning design studios that engage multiple forms of intelligence.

About the Illustrator

Becky Green has many more wrinkles than her avatar suggests, and she celebrates that illusion as just another perk of doodling. She cares deeply about the magic that happens when words and images are paired to create meaning, and she infuses her English and social studies classrooms with opportunities to write, draw, create, and play.

She's taught in Southeast Asia, North America, and virtual classrooms worldwide. Wherever you are on the globe, Becky would love to hear from you and celebrate the good things you're learning and creating.

doodle2learn.com